Knowledge *Blaster!* Guide to

Myth and Legend

Yucca Road Productions

ISBN   9781452860954

Cover design by YRP staff
Revised in 2020
Published in the United States by Yucca
Road Productions
Printed in the United States of America

Dear Reader,

The *Knowledge BLASTER!* Series consists of books of general and academic interest, written with the specific intention of compressing a great mountain of available information into an easily digestible morsel. Every attempt has been made to simplify unwieldy material.

Where feasible, the books are patterned in an efficient question-and-answer mode in which answers become meaningful extensions of helpful, information-packed questions.

We hope you use this reference work as a launch pad to propel yourself into more in-depth studies. However, if you find this little book provides all the information you need, then consider your knowledge...
Blasted!

Knowledge BLASTER! Series
American History
Art History
Food and Drink
Geography and Travel
Literature
Movies
Music
Mythology
Sports
Weight Training and Total Fitness
World History

Yucca Road Productions

Knowledge BLASTER! Guide to **Myth and Legend** is a
brief and concise compendium of the best-known events,
characters, and places of legend. Each section lists in
alphabetical order those that were particular to the region.

Contents

Greek Myths and Legends

The Greek gods were the superheroes of their day, displaying incredible strengths and powers along with human-like quirks and frailties of character.

As a matter of convenience, the entries in this book often refer to the characters and events in them as if they were real. Only in those cases where mention is made of the actuality of an event or character should they be considered as real people or occurrences.

Achilles: Greatest of the Greek warriors in Homer's 3,000 year-old Iliad, the story of war against the city of Troy. When Achilles was a baby, his mother, Thetis, had a vision that he would be killed in battle, and so, holding him by one of his heels, she dipped him in the magic river Styx to make him invincible. The war with Troy began when Achilles reached manhood; and he proved himself a mighty warrior; he even chased the Trojan champion, Hector, around the walls of the city. During one battle, he was struck in the heel— the only part of his body that was not immersed in the Styx— and died. Because of this, a person's weakest point has been called his "Achilles' heel."

Adonis: An incredibly handsome young Greek, Adonis attracted the goddess Aphrodite. She tried to dissuade him from hunting, but he ignored her advice and was killed on a hunt by a wild boar. Appalled at the prospect of Adonis spending eternity in the underworld, Aphrodite persuaded the other gods to allow him to come up to earth for six months out of every year. She changed his blood into a flower, the anemone, and each year, the blooming of the anemone signals the return of Adonis from the underworld.

Aeolus: The Greek god of the winds. His name was given to a musical instrument, the aeolian harp, because the strings of the instrument are played by blowing air across them instead of plucking them.

Aegisthus: See the article on Agamemnon.

Agamemnon: King of Mycenae in ancient Greece, he was commander-in-chief of the Greek forces throughout the Trojan Wars. While Agamemnon was away, his wife Clytemnestra fell in love with Aegisthus, a Greek prince. This couple murdered Agamemnon on his return. His son, Orestes, later avenged his death by killing both Clytemnestra and Aegisthus. See also the article on Electra.

Ajax: In the story of the Trojan Wars, there were two Greek warriors named Ajax. Only Achilles was a greater warrior than "Ajax the Greater." Upon Achilles' death, this Ajax wanted his armor, but it was given to Ulysses and Ajax killed himself.

"Ajax the Less" was known to be second only to Achilles as a fast and sure-footed runner. He was struck down by a bolt of lightning for offending the gods.

Amazons: In Greek myth, these women warriors lived in a country on the Mediterranean Sea. Strong and swift, they allowed no men in their nation and battled against the men of other nations. Once each year the Amazons visited another country, and the men of the chosen country became fathers of the Amazon children (the boys were not kept, of course.)

Andromeda: A princess of Ethiopia, daughter of Cepheus and Cassiopeia. Her mother's claim that Andromeda's beauty was greater than that of the nereids (sea nymphs) angered Poseidon, who sent a sea monster that could only be appeased by her sacrifice. Perseus slew the monster and married Andromeda.

Apollo (or Phoebus Apollo): Greek god of music, poetry, light, and healing, Apollo was considered the friend and advisor of mankind. He was the son of Zeus and second in importance only to him. Artemis, the moon goddess, was his twin sister.

Apollo was the father of Asclepius, god of healing and medicine. Animals sacred to Apollo and under his special protection were the wolf, raven, swan, mouse, and deer. The nine Muses, who ruled over all the arts, usually attended him.

Statues usually depict Apollo as young and handsome, wearing a laurel wreath on his head and carrying a lyre. The most famous of these is in Belvedere (a part of the Vatican) in Rome.

Ares: God of war (Roman Mars). A rather cruel god, Ares delighted in the horror and bloodshed of battle.

Artemis: Daughter of Zeus and Leto, twin sister of Apollo. She was goddess of the moon and hunting, and protector of young animals. Artemis never married, and the priests and priestesses in temples devoted to her were not allowed to marry. (Roman Diana.)

Athena, or Pallas Athena (Roman Minerva): Goddess of heroism and wisdom, and patron of all womanly arts, such as spinning, sewing, and weaving. She was not born in the usual way; she sprang fully-grown and armored from the forehead of Zeus.

The most beautiful temple of Athens, the Parthenon on the hill called the Acropolis, was dedicated to Athena.

Athenaeum: The name given to any ancient Greek temple honoring Athena. Because the name is so closely associated with learning, a school or literary club or magazine is often called Athenaeum.

Atlantis: Legendary "lost island" usually said to have existed, and disappeared, in the Atlantic Ocean (or Mediterranean Sea). The Greek philosopher Plato wrote the story of the legend in 375 BC.

Poseidon, god of the sea, created the island and the nine rings of land that surrounded it for Cleito, his beloved. The king and people of Atlantis descended from the children of these two.

A utopian isle of serenity and wealth, its houses had roofs of gleaming red copper, and its two temples, surrounded by walls of silver and gold, had roofs of ivory.

In 1967, a city was found, near Greece, that had been buried by a volcanic eruption around 1500 BC. Archaeologists speculate that this might be the lost city.

Atlas: One of the Titans, a race of giants who were the ancestors of the Greek gods, ruling the world until their defeat by the Greek gods. To keep them from ever regaining power, the Titans were punished in various ways; Atlas was made to hold the world on his shoulders.

Ancient maps were drawn with pictures of Atlas holding the earth, and this practice led to the custom of calling books of maps, atlases.

Bellerophon: Hero who accomplished seemingly impossible tasks given to him by King Iobates. With the help of the winged horse Pegasus, Bellerophon killed the monster Chimera.

Made vain by his success, Bellerophon attempted to ride

Pegasus to Mount Olympus but was thrown, crippled and blinded as punishment for his vanity. See also the article on Pegasus.

Cadmus: In Greek mythology, Cadmus founded the city of Thebes. After killing a sacred dragon, he pulled out the dragon's teeth and planted them in the ground, like seeds. From each tooth sprang up a soldier, and these became the ancestors of the citizens of Thebes. Ares, god of war, was angry at Cadmus for slaying the sacred dragon and caused many bad things to befall him and his family.

Cadmus was also honored as the inventor of the alphabet.

Calliope: The muse of epic poetry.

Cassandra: A beautiful princess with whom the god Apollo fell in love. After giving to her the power of prophecy, Apollo found that Cassandra did not return his love and, in anger, vowed that no one would believe her predictions. Cassandra correctly foresaw the fall of the city of Troy to the Greeks, but her warnings were ignored.

Castor and Pollux: Twin sons of Leda (the Queen of Sparta) and Zeus, according to one legend. Castor and Pollux were enormous men and overwhelming warriors. Castor was a great horseman, and Pollux was a feared boxer. Besides appearing in battle to aid the side that they had chosen, they were said to rescue sailors in peril.

Centaur: With the head, arms, and trunk of a man and the body, legs and tail of a horse, these wild creatures were great hunters, and friendly to men. A very wise centaur, Chiron, taught Achilles and Aesculapius and other heroes about hunting, medicine, and music. Chiron is said to have raised Jason.

Cerberus: Guardian of the entrance to the underworld, this three-headed dog had the tail of a serpent and a mane made of the heads of snakes. He ensured that no living person could enter the underworld and that no spirits of the dead could leave.

The ancient Greeks and Romans placed cakes in the hands of their dead before burial, as a bribe to Cerberus to assure safe passage.

Chaos: The unfathomable empty space from which all things arose. Gaea (earth) sprang from Chaos and became the mother of all things.

Charon: Usually depicted as an ugly old man, this Greek character ferried the spirits of the dead across the rivers of Archeron and Styx on their journey to the underworld. Charon demanded a fee for his services, and so the Greeks would place a coin in the mouth of the deceased, to pay the ferryman.

Charybdis: See the article on Scylla and Charybdis.

Chiron: Centaur who raised Jason and taught Achilles. See articles on centaur and Jason.

Circe: Daughter of the sun god Helios, Circe lived in a palace on the island of Aeaea and had the power to change men into beasts.

In Homer's *Odyssey*, Ulysses (the Latin name for Odysseus) and his soldiers were sailing home from the Trojan War and stopped off at Aeaea. Ulysses' men were invited by Circe to dine at her palace, and all but one, Eurylochus, agreed. After the feast, Circe turned them all into swine, but Eurylochus saw what had happened and rushed back to the ship to tell Ulysses. The god Hermes appeared and told Ulysses to threaten Circe in order to make her return his men to their normal state. This approach worked, and gained the respect of the sorceress. Ulysses and his men then stayed for a year on the island.

Clio: The muse of history.

Croesus: A real king of Lydia, famous for his great wealth, whose story has become mixed with legend. He extended his kingdom on Asia Minor to include Phrygia, which had been the home of Midas of the legendary "golden touch." It is said that Croesus' wealth came from the golden sands of the river in which Midas washed away his cursed "touch," the river called Pactolus (Baguli.)

When Lydia was threatened by Cyrus, King of Persia, Croesus consulted the Oracle at Delphi, in Greece. The Oracle told him that he would destroy a great empire, and Croesus thought this meant that he would conquer Persia. Acting on this prediction, he attacked the forces of Cyrus, but his own army was insufficient. His troops were defeated, his capital was captured, and there was never another king of Lydia. He had, indeed, destroyed a great empire— his own.

Cronos: God of time and chief of the Titans. Having dethroned his own father, Cronos reacted with swift brutality when told that his own son would someday dethrone him— he swallowed his children. However, one son escaped; Zeus led a great war against the Titans and managed to dethrone his father.

As Father Time, Cronos is pictured with a scythe and an hourglass. He is also the father of Demeter (Roman Ceres).

Cyclops (plural Cyclopes): Fierce, one-eyed giants who sometimes ate men. They made the lightning bolts that Zeus hurled across the sky.

See the articles on *Odyssey* and Polyphemus.

Daedalus: An artist and inventor who made great statues, temples, and ships. He invented many carpenter's tools. Daedalus and his son, Icarus, were imprisoned at one point. To escape, they built two pairs of wings from bird feathers held together with wax. On the escape flight, Icarus flew too close to the sun, causing the wax to melt. He fell into the sea and drowned. Daedalus was more careful, and returned safely.

The story or Icarus is used as a warning against reckless behavior.

Damocles: Many times Damocles had told Dionysius the Elder, ruler of Sicily, how fortunate he was to be rich and powerful. To show Damocles that there was a price to be paid for his wealth and power, Dionysius invited him to a great feast. At first, Damocles enjoyed the luxury and spectacle, but then he noticed a sword above his head, suspended by a single thread. Though he was fearful throughout the rest of the feast, he had learned of the constant worry of being a ruler.

Dionysius was a real person, and Sicily is a real island. It is not known whether the legend of Damocles is based on fact.

Damon and Pythias: Friends who were willing to give up their lives for each other. As followers of the Greek teacher Pythagorus, these two learned the highest rules of conduct and action.

Dionysius I, cruel ruler of Syracuse on the island of Sicily, condemned Pythias to death for plotting against him. Damon offered to stay in prison in his place, so that Pythias could visit his family one last time. As the time of execution approached,

Pythias was unexpectedly delayed, and it seemed that Damon would be killed in his place. Pythias returned just in time, and then each of the friends asked to die so that the other could go free. Dionysius was so impressed by this gesture that he pardoned both of the friends.

Danae: Beautiful daughter of King Acrisius. When Acrisius was told by an oracle that his grandson would kill him, he shut away Danae so that she could have no children. Zeus, who loved her, turned himself into a shower of gold and visited her. When Danae had a son from this union, Acrisius put them both to sea in a large box, hoping that they would drown. However, they drifted safely to an island where the son, Perseus, grew to be a great hero. In an athletic contest, Perseus threw a discus, which accidentally struck Acrisius in the foot and caused his death, proving the oracle's prediction. Perseus also slew Medusa. See the article on the Gorgons.

Danaides: King Danaus of Libya had fifty daughters, called the Danaides. The fifty sons of his brother, Aegyptus, tried to overthrow Danaus, who fled with his daughters. Later, when the sons wanted to marry his girls, he agreed but secretly ordered the daughters to kill their new husbands on the wedding night. All but one of the girls obeyed, chopping off the men's heads with swords and throwing them into the river. After death, the daughters were punished in the underworld by forever drawing water from a well in sieves.

Daphne: A beautiful nature spirit, or nymph. She was the first girl with whom Apollo fell in love, but Daphne ran away from him. As she was chased near her father's river, she called out for help and was changed into a laurel tree. Greatly saddened, Apollo then claimed laurel trees as sacred to him, and wore on his head a crown of laurel leaves.

The laurel wreath has long been used as a symbol of victory (or peace.)

Daphnis: A handsome shepherd, much favored by the Greek goddesses, whose sweetheart was a nymph. In one version of the myth, Daphnis was so faithful to his lover that not even Aphrodite could win him away, but in another version he was unfaithful, and the nymph blinded him (or turned him into stone.)

Lityerses, a cruel farmer who always killed those who could not reap as much grain as he could, beat Daphnis in such a contest, but the gods saved Daphnis and killed Lityerses instead.

Daphnis is credited with creating the first songs about shepherds and herdsmen.

Delphi, Oracle of: The voice of a god who gave people advice. The Temple of Delphi was near Mount Parnassus, and here a priestess would allow a god (most say Apollo) to speak through her in response to questions asked of her. There was a crack in the floor of the temple, just over a stream of water called the Cassotis which flowed beneath the building. The priestess seated herself over this crack, from which steam rose, and received the words of Apollo from the steam. Often, the answers were difficult to understand, and at times a priest would try to interpret them.

See the article on Croesus.

Demeter: Goddess of farming and the harvest. (Roman Ceres.)

Deucalion and Pyrrha: King and Queen of Phthia. When Zeus caused a great flood, they alone survived drowning, by floating in a ship for nine days and nights. They landed atop

Mount Parnassus. When the waters receded, Deucalion prayed to Zeus to restore the people, and Zeus told him to walk along casting his mother's bones behind him. Figuring that this meant the stones of "Mother Earth," the pair dropped stones as they walked. The stones dropped by Deucalion turned into men, and those dropped by Pyrrha turned into women.

Dionysius: Name of rulers on Sicily.
See the articles on Damocles and Damon and Pythias.

Dionysus: God of grapes and wine, son of Zeus and the human woman, Semele. To the Greeks, he was also god of the theater, and they performed their plays in outdoor theaters that were built in his honor.
Festivals in his honor were called Dionysia. (Roman Bacchus, whose festivals were called Bacchanalia.

Dioscuri: The inclusive name for twins Castor and Pollux.

Dryads: Nymphs, lovely maidens who lived in trees. They were friendly to humans, but hated and punished those who destroyed trees for no reason.

Echo: A nymph who once helped Zeus by chattering away at his wife, Hera, so that she would not notice a transgression that he was committing behind her back. As punishment, Echo lost the power to speak her own thoughts, and could only repeat the words of others. She fell in love with the beautiful young man, Narcissus, but as her love was not returned, she pined away until there was nothing left of her but her voice.

Electra: Daughter of Agamemnon (king of Mycenae) and Clytemnestra, and sister of Orestes. When Agamemnon returned from the Trojan Wars and was murdered by his wife and her lover, Electra had Orestes sent far away for his own protection. She plotted to avenge her father, and, when Orestes grew up and returned home with a friend, she helped the pair kill Clytemnestra and Aegisthus, the lover. Later, she married Orestes' friend, Pyiades.

Elysian Fields: A beautiful and happy place where good men went after they died.

Endymion: A young shepherd who was so handsome that Selene, goddess of the moon, fell in love with him. She kissed him, and thereafter Endymion slept forever, with Selene watching over him and caring for his sheep. Every night she would look over him and kiss him with soft light.

Eos (Roman Aurora): "Rosy-fingered" goddess of the dawn and mother of the winds and stars. She drove a chariot across the sky to announce the arrival of the sun.

In love with the Trojan prince Tithonus, Eos asked Zeus to grant eternal life to the prince. This was done. However, she forgot to ask also that Tithonus remain young, and so he grew older and older and finally withered away until only his voice was left.

Erato: The muse of love poetry.

Erinyes: See the article on the Furies.

Eris: Goddess of discord and sister of Ares, the war god. Becoming angry when all of the gods and goddesses except her were invited to a great feast, she threw a beautiful golden apple into the midst of the guests. The apple was inscribed with the words, "To the fairest," and three of the goddesses (each thinking that she was the most beautiful) claimed it as their own. The Trojan prince Paris was asked to decide which goddess was the fairest. His choice of Aphrodite later led to the Trojan War.

See the articles on Paris and the Trojan War.

Eros: God of love (Roman Cupid). Son of Aphrodite and Ares, he is usually depicted as a winged youth armed with bow and arrows.

Eumenides: See the article on the Furies.

Europa: A princess of Greek myth. Zeus took the form of a white bull and swam, with Europa on his back, to Crete, an island south of Greece. He gave her a dog that never lost its prey, a bronze man (Talos), and a spear that never missed its target. Europa had three sons by Zeus and later married the king of Crete.

After her death, Europa was worshiped as the goddess of the earth.

Euryale: See the article on Gorgons.

Euterpe: The muse of lyric poetry.

Furies (or Erinyes): Avenging goddesses who punished not only criminals, but those who disobeyed their parents or showed disrespect for their elders, etc. Living deep in the nether world, they had snakes in their hair and blood dripping from their eyes.

The Eumenides were also Furies, but they dispensed justice.

Ganymede: Son of the king of Troy, he was the most beautiful man on earth. Zeus thought Ganymede was so handsome that he should be a god, and so he took the form of an eagle, scooped up the young man, and took him to Mount Olympus. As a cup bearer, Ganymede served water and wine to the gods, and was a kind of god himself. He was called the source of all the earth's waters and protector of the Nile River in Egypt.

Golden Fleece: A ram (male sheep) whose fleece was made of gold. After being killed by the god Aeolus for carrying away two of his grandchildren, the ram was skinned and the Golden Fleece was guarded by a dragon. See the article on Jason.

Gordian knot: The complicated knot that Gordius used to tie the yoke to his wagon. An oracle had foretold that the people of Phrygia would know their next king by his arrival in a wagon. When Gordius, a poor peasant, came to the marketplace in such a wagon, the people proclaimed him their king. Grateful for his good fortune, Gordius dedicated his wagon to Zeus.

The oracle had also foretold that the man who could loosen the knot that held this wagon's yoke would become ruler of all Asia. Alexander the Great, a real person, is said to have come to the city and simply slashed the knot with his sword. Though Alexander may not have actually done this, in reality, he did go on to conquer Asia.

Gorgons: Three women with hair of snakes, sharp claws, and huge teeth. Named Stheno, Medusa, and Euryale, they were so horrible to see that anyone who looked upon them was instantly turned to stone. A Greek hero named Perseus chopped off the bead of Medusa with his sword, while looking at her reflection in his polished shield. He offered the head to Athena, the goddess who had given him the shield.

Harpies: Goddesses of the storms who played mean tricks on men. They were ugly creatures with either human faces or birds' heads, with animal ears, and wings and bodies covered with feathers. Their arms and legs were that of a human, but they had claws instead of hands and birds' feet.

In literature, such as the stories of the Iliad and the Odyssey, harpies represent dangers or evils which the heroes must overcome.

Hebe: Goddess of youth, daughter of Zeus and Hera, and handmaiden (helper) of the gods. At meals, she would fill the gods' cups with nectar. She helped the war god to don his armor, and she helped Hera to harness her horses to her chariot. She married the hero Heracles when he was made a god.

In some stories, Hebe made old people young again.

Hecate: A goddess of the underworld. She was the goddess of magic and teacher of witches and sorcerers. She sent out spirits and demons at night, and sometimes she would haunt graveyards and crossroads. On these occasions, she would take her dogs, which caused the dogs of the Greeks to howl at night when Hecate was nearby.

Hector: Eldest son of King Priam and Queen Hecuba, of Troy. He was the great leader of the Trojan army in the wars against the Greeks, and it was said that Troy could not be defeated while Hector lived. He was slain by Achilles, who dragged his body behind a chariot. Achilles would not return the body to the Trojans until King Priam had pleaded and given him many fine gifts. Shortly after Hector's death, Troy was defeated.

Helen of Troy: The most beautiful woman in the world, married to a Greek prince named Menelaus. She was stolen by

Paris, a prince of Troy, beginning the Trojan Wars. Eventually, Troy was destroyed by the Greeks, and Helen was returned to her husband.

Helios: The sun god and father of Phaeton and Circe. Apollo was also called the sun god. See the articles on Phaeton and Circe.

Hellesponte: The strait of water between Europe and Asia Minor, now called the Dardanelles.

Hercules: The strongest man in the world, son of Zeus and the human woman, Alcmene. As a baby, he killed a great serpent that threatened him in his cradle. Zeus' wife, Hera, was jealous of Hercules because he was the product of Zeus' affair with another woman, and so she tricked Hercules into performing tasks that, she thought, would cause his failure or death. These tasks were known as the Twelve Labors of Hercules, and were:
1.   To destroy the lion of Nemes. Hercules strangled it with his bare hands.
2.   To kill the Lernean hydra, a monster with nine heads, each of which would regenerate when cut off. He obtained a torch from his nephew, Iolaus, which he used to burn the roots of each head as he cut it off. (See the article on hydra.)
3.   To capture the golden-horned, bronze-hoofed Arcadian stag, renowned for its speed. He caught it after a year of pursuit.
4.   To capture a rampaging wild boar. After a chase through deep snow, Hercules netted the beast.
5.   To clean the stables where three thousand oxen, belonging to King Augeas of Elis, had lived for thirty years. Diverting the course of two rivers to run through the stables, Hercules washed them clean in a single day.
6.   To rid the city of Stymphalus of man-eating birds that

lived nearby. After sneaking up on the birds, Hercules startled them by shaking a rattle and shot them with bow and arrow as they flew away.

7.   To capture a beautiful bull which had been made mad by Poseidon, the sea god. He did so, and carried the live bull back on his shoulders.

8.   To catch the flesh-eating mares of Diomedes, King of Thrace. By feeding them on the flesh of their own master, Hercules tamed the mares.

9.   To acquire the girdle (belt) of the Queen of the Amazons, Hippolyta. He killed the queen and took her belt.

10.   To destroy Geryon, the three-bodied monster, and take his oxen to Argos. Hercules not only accomplished this task, but, on his way, built a pillar on either side of the Strait of Gibraltar, which are still called the Pillars of Hercules.

11.   To take the golden apples from the garden of the Hesperides. Hercules relieved the giant Atlas of his job of holding the world on his shoulders, while Atlas got the apples for him.

12.   To bring Cerberus, the three-headed dog, back from the underworld. Once this was accomplished, Hercules was freed from his labors.

Hermes (Roman Mercury): Messenger of the gods and patron of astronomy, music, gymnastics, and military tactics. To the Romans, Mercury was also god of trade and profits. He invented the lyre and the flute.

To speed him on his way, he wore a winged cap and wings on his heels. His winged staff, with two serpents winding around it, was called a caduceus, and is today used as the symbol for the practice of medicine.

Hero and Leander: Doomed lovers who lived on opposite banks of the Hellespont (the strait of water which separates

Europe and Asia Minor, now called the Dardanelles). The lady Hero was a priestess at Sestos in a temple to Aphrodite. Leander, of Abydos, met her at a festival in the temple, and the two fell in love.

Every night, Hero would light a lamp in a window of the tower to guide Leander as he swam across the Hellespont, a distance of three or four miles. On one occasion, the lamp was blown out in a storm. Leander lost his way and drowned in the rough sea. His body was washed ashore in the morning, and the grieving Hero dove from her tower into the water, where she drowned.

Hesperides: The four daughters of Atlas and Hesperia, guardians of the golden apples that were stolen by Hercules as one of the Twelve Labors. Gaea, goddess of the earth, had presented the apples as a wedding present to Zeus and Hera. The Hesperides were named Agle, Arethusa, Erytheia, and Hesperia.

Hippolyta: An Amazon queen. See the article on Hercules.

Hydra: A terrible nine-headed water snake that inhabited the marshes of Lerna, a part of Greece. When one head was cut off, two immediately grew in its place, and the ninth head was immortal. Its breath brought instant death to any who inhaled it. The hydra was slain by Hercules, who buried the immortal head under a giant rock. See the article on Hercules.

Icarus: Daedalus' son who escaped from Crete on wings of wax and feathers. He flew too close to the sun, the wax melted, and he plunged into the sea and drowned.
    See the article on Daedalus.

Iliad: The story, told by the Greek poet Homer, of the Trojan
Wars and the Greek hero Achilles.

See the articles on Achilles, Agamemnon, Helen of Troy,
Hector, Clyternnestra, and the Trojan Wars.

Io: One of Zeus' many love interests. After their romance, Io
gave birth to a son, Bpaphus. Hera, wife of Zeus, was jealous
of her. To protect her from Hera's wrath, Zeus changed Io into
a white heifer (young cow). Discovering her true identity,
Hera sent a stinging gadfly to torment her. After roving
through many lands, lo was returned to human form on the
banks of the Nile.

In another story, Io married the king of Egypt, and she
became the goddess Isis.

Jason: Son of Aeson, a king who was overthrown by his
brother, Pelias. For his own protection, Jason was given to a
centaur, Chiron, and raised by him. In adulthood, Jason
returned to claim his father's throne, and Pelias agreed to
surrender it if Jason would bring him the Golden Fleece.
The Golden Fleece was kept in the faraway land of Colchis
and guarded by a mighty dragon, and so Jason gathered a crew
of heroic men and set off on his ship, the Argo. The ship had a
magic beam on its bow that could talk. Since the ship was
called Argo, and "naut" means sailor, the crewmen were called
"Argonauts."

On Colchis, Jason married a princess named Medea, who
helped him to get the Fleece. On returning home, Jason
learned that Pelias had killed his father. Medea tricked Pelias'
daughters into killing the old man, but, for this crime, both
Jason and Medea were banished. In Corinth, Jason fell in love
with another princess, Creusa, and soon left Medea for this
new love. Seeking revenge, Medea slew Creusa and killed her

own children by Jason. In some tellings of this story, Jason then killed himself.

Labyrinth: A large, complex tunnel, full of twists and turns so that none who entered could ever find their way out. It was built by Daedalus on the island of Crete and held the Minotaur, a fierce creature with a bull's head and a human body. The Minotaur required the sacrifice of seven boys and seven girls each year.

　　Sent to Crete to destroy the Minotaur, the Greek hero Theseus obtained a long thread from Ariadne, daughter of the king. Theseus tied one end of the string to the entrance to the labyrinth. He entered, found the Minotaur and killed him, and followed the string back out.

Laocoon: A priest of Troy who advised his people to be suspicious about anything Greek, even their gifts. The Trojan Wars had gone on for many years, when, suddenly, the Greeks sailed away, leaving only a wooden horse at the gate to the city. When Laocoon issued his warning to beware of this seemingly harmless gift, two huge serpents rose from the sea, came ashore, and entwined Laocoon and his two sons, killing them. Taking this as a god-given sign that Laocoon had been wrong, the Trojans pulled the wooden horse into the city.

　　At night, a small band of Greek warriors (who were hidden inside the horse,) crept out and opened the gates of the city. Since the war ships had returned in secret, the main body of the Greek force was ready to enter the city. The sleeping Trojans were overwhelmed.

Lethe: One of the five rivers of the underworld, or Hades. Before the spirits of the dead could enter Hades, they had to forget all that had gone on before. One sip from the Lethe, River of Forgetfulness, would make them forget. By the same token, a spirit that was destined to live again would drink from the Lethe to forget about Hades.

Lotus Eaters: People on the northern coast of Africa who, according to the myth, ate nothing but the lotus plant.

Supposedly, the lotus made them forget all their sorrows and live happy, lazy lives. See the article on the Odyssey.

Lydia: See the article on Croesus.

Medea: Wife of Jason who helped him retrieve the Golden Fleece. See the articles on Jason and the Golden Fleece.

Medusa: Awful Gorgon slain by Perseus. See the article on the Gorgons.

Melpomene: The muse of tragedy.

Memnon: An Ethiopian king who led an army to help the Trojans in their war against the Greeks. Almost immediately after slaying the Greek warrior Antilochus, Memnon himself was killed by Achilles.

A sixty foot high statue of Memnon was erected in Thebes, Egypt. The eerie sound of the stone expanding in the morning sun caused the statue to be called "the vocal Memnon."

Midas: King of a Greek country called Phrygia. In return for a favor, the god Dionysus agreed to grant Midas any wish. He wished that everything he touched would turn to gold. Soon, Midas found that even the food that he wanted to eat turned to gold, and he almost starved. He could not touch an animal or person, for fear that they would be changed to golden statues. He begged Dionysus to take back his power, and was instructed to bathe in the River Pactolus. This he did, the power was removed, and the sands of the river turned to gold.

Another time, Midas judged a musical contest between the gods Apollo and Pan. His ruling that Pan had won the contest so angered Apollo that he changed Midas' ears to that of an ass. Midas hid his huge ears under a cap, but he had to take his cap off to get his hair cut. The servant who cut his hair, afraid to tell anyone, dug a hole in the ground and whispered into the hole, "The king has donkey's ears." Reeds grew up from the ground there, and whispered the servant's words in the wind.

Another story says that King Midas later killed himself by drinking ox blood.

Minotaur: Half-man, half-bull creature belonging to King Minos of Crete. It lived in the labyrinth and was slain by Theseus. See the article on labyrinth.

Muses: Nine daughters of Zeus and Mnemosyne (goddess of memory). They were goddesses of music, poetry, and the arts. With Apollo as their leader, they played instruments and sang at feasts.
They were:
· Calliope, the muse of epic poetry
· Clio, the muse of history
· Erato, the muse of love poetry
· Euterpe, the muse of lyric poetry
· Melpomene, the muse of tragedy
· Polyhymnia, the muse of oratory and solemn song
· Terpsichore, the muse of dancing
· Thalia, the muse of comedy, and
· Urania, the muse of astronomy.

Naiads: Water nymphs. They were long-haired maidens, young and beautiful, who lived in rivers and lakes and fountains. They had the power to cure sick people, and often inspired poets and soothsayers who drank from their waters.

Narcissus: A handsome young man who was loved by many nymphs, but loved no one. One day he glanced his own reflection in a pool of still water and fell in love with himself (or his reflection). He longed for himself so badly that, it is said, he died of love.

One legend says that the narcissus plant sprang from his body. Like him, the blossom is beautiful but for a short while.

See the article on Echo.

Nectar: Drink of the gods. A delicious drink with great powers, it made the gods immortal, forever young, and beautiful.

Although **ambrosia** is sometimes referred to in the stories as being the same as nectar, usually ambrosia meant the food that was eaten by the gods.

Nemesis: Goddess who imposed punishment on those who made the gods angry.

Niobe: Daughter of Tantalus, king of Lydia. With her husband Amphion, king of Thebes, she had six sons and six daughters, of whom she was very proud. Her boast that she had more children than Leto (mother of Apollo and Artemis) reached the ears of the two gods and angered them. Considering her brag an insult to their mother, Apollo and Artemis killed all of Niobe's children, one at a time, and turned Niobe to a statue of stone. Even in this condition, her sadness was so great that the statue wept silent tears of sorrow.

Nymphs: Beautiful goddesses that were most like humans, and could marry men. Fond of dancing and hunting, nymphs lived in rivers and oceans, forests and mountains. They were the guardians of the beautiful things of nature: oreads of mountains, naiads of bodies of fresh water, nereids of the Mediterranean Sea, oceanids of the ocean, and dryads of trees. Hamadryads lived and died with a particular tree.

***Odyssey*:** Greek poet Homer's story of Odysseus, or Ulysses, a hero of the Trojan Wars, and his voyage home to the Greek kingdom of Ithaca at war's end. Landing in Ismarus, home of the Ciconians, Odysseus and his men tried to confiscate some of the country's wealth, but were driven off by an attack of the Ciconians in which many of the Greeks were killed. Journeying on, they were blown by a storm to the land of the Lotus Eaters, who drugged themselves into a state of slovenly happiness on the lotus plant. Here, Odysseus had to force his men to return to the ship.

On the island of Sicily, they encountered the Cyclops, a one-eyed giant who devoured several of Odysseus' men. The escape was made after Odysseus put out the giant's one eye. On the island of the sorceress Circe, some of the sailors were turned into pigs (see article on Circe), but the god Mercury helped Odysseus, and the men remained for a time with Circe.

After other adventures, in which all the men except Odysseus were killed, the hero sailed alone to an island where Calypso, a daughter of Atlas, lived. His ship wrecked, he was stranded on the island for seven years. Then, with the help of Mercury, he returned to his home. His long-faithful wife, Penelope, believing Odysseus dead, was being courted by several young men of Ithaca. In the end, Odysseus routed them and was reunited with Penelope.

Oedipus: Son of Laius, king of Thebes, and Jacosta. It was foretold that Oedipus would kill his father. To negate this prophecy, Laius had his son put on a mountain to die, but

Oedipus was saved, and raised by the king of Corinth. When he was gown, it was foretold that not only would he kill his father but marry his own mother. Thinking that the king of Corinth was his real father, Oedipus left the kingdom. Traveling by chance toward Thebes, he met Laius, who blocked his path. In a fit of temper, Oedipus killed Laius. He journeyed on to Thebes. There he met Laius' widow, Jacosta, fell in love with her, and soon married her. Later discovering that he had, indeed, killed his father and married his mother, Oedipus punished himself by putting out his eyes. Jacosta killed herself.

Oracle: A place at which the gods spoke to human beings. Early stories used the term to refer to the message itself, but later it came to mean the place. Oracles in different places were attended by different gods and used different means of delivering advice in answer to men's questions. Sometimes the message was given through a person in a trance, sometimes through a dream, and sometimes through a natural occurrence which was taken as a sign. Often a priest would receive the message in strange words which he would then interpret. See Delphi, Oracle of.

Orestes: Avenging son of Agamemnon.
See the articles on Agamemnon, Clytemnestra, and Electra.

Orion: A mighty hunter. He is usually pictured with sword raised and shield extended in front, awaiting the charge of Taurus, the bull.

Orpheus: Son of Apollo and Calliope, the Muse of epic poetry. He was taught music by the Muses. On a lyre given to Orpheus by Apollo, he made music so beautiful that wild beasts who heard it became tame.

Orpheus fell in love with Eurydice, a beautiful nymph, and on her death from a snake bite, he was so overcome with sorrow that he journeyed to Hades to find her. Pluto, ruler of Hades, was astounded by the beauty of Orpheus' music. He agreed to send Eurydice back to the land of the living on the condition that Orpheus would not look back at her until they had reached the upper world. Orpheus agreed, and the pair began their journey. However, just before they reached the upper world, Orpheus did look back at Eurydice, and she vanished forever.

In his great sadness, Orpheus was cruel to the women of Thrace, and they killed him. When he was buried, a nightingale came to sing over his grave.

Pan: God of fishermen and hunters, he watched over shepherds and their flocks. Pan had the body and head of a man and the beard, horns, and feet of a goat. He lived in rocky caves, played songs on a shepherd's pipe, and danced merrily with pretty nymphs. He was known for his loud voice, which would frighten those who traveled the woods on dark nights. Pan was a favorite of all the gods, especially Dionysus, god of wine.

Pandora: In Greek mythology, the first woman. Pandora was created by Zeus and sent to Prometheus and his brother, Epimetheus. In some stories, she was sent as a punishment to Prometheus because he had given fire to man. Another version claims that she was sent by Zeus as a blessing to man. Each of the gods gave her a wonderful gift.

She married Epimetheus and caused him great trouble. He had a box which contained all of the evils of the world (including hatred, envy, and disease) and also hope. Her curiosity led Pandora to open the box, and all the evils flew out to beset man; hope was all that remained in the box. From that time onward, mankind was made to suffer many misfortunes but, through them all, retained hope.

Paris: Son of Priam, who was King of Troy. As a baby, Paris was left on a lonely mountain by his parents because it had been predicted that he would cause the ruin of Troy. He was found and raised by a shepherd.

Paris was chosen to settle an argument between Aphrodite, Hera, and Athena as to which goddess was most beautiful. The prize was to be a golden apple (see the article on Eris). Paris chose Aphrodite. As a reward, he was sent by her to the home of the Greek prince Menelaus, because the prince's wife, Helen, was the most beautiful woman in the world. Paris stole Helen and took her to Troy, thus beginning the Trojan Wars. See the article on the Trojan Wars.

Pegasus: Winged horse belonging to the Greek hero Bellerophon. Pegasus sprang from the neck of the dying Gorgon Medusa. After being caught and tamed by Athena, Pegasus was given to the muses. The horse pawed at the earth, and the fountain of inspiration, called the Hippocrene, bubbled up. Poets rode to the land of inspiration on Pegasus.

Penelope: Faithful wife of Odysseus. See the article on the *Odyssey*.

Perseus: Son of Zeus and Danae. Perseus killed Medusa, looking at her reflection in his polished shield while cutting off her head with his sword.

He married Andromeda after rescuing the maiden from a sea monster.

See the articles on Andromeda, Danae, and the Gorgons.

Phaeton: Son of Helios (the sun god). After persistently begging his father to be allowed to drive the chariot of the sun across the sky, Phaeton was granted his wish. Realizing too late that he was not strong enough to control the chariot, he plunged to earth— chariot, sun, and all. The earth seemed near destruction; the rivers dried up, and deserts were formed from fertile farmlands. At the last moment, Zeus killed Phaeton with a thunderbolt, and the earth was saved.

Pleiades: Seven daughters of Atlas. They were turned into stars, and the constellation they formed was called "the Pleiades," or "the Seven Sisters."

Pluto: Ruler of the underworld, or Hades. Pluto married Persephone, daughter of the goddess of grain. For six months each year (spring and summer), Pluto let his wife rejoin her mother, so that the goddess would let the grain grow, to feed the humans.

Polyhymnia: Muse of oratory and solemn song.

Polyphemus: Cyclops who imprisoned Odysseus and his men in a cave. Polyphemus was made drunk and blinded to facilitate their escape.

Poseidon: God of the sea. (Roman Neptune.)

Priam: King of Troy in Homer's poem, the *Iliad*. Priam's wife was Hecuba. One of their sons, Paris, started the Trojan Wars by stealing the most beautiful woman in the world, Helen, from the Greek prince who was her husband. Another son, Hector, was killed by the Greek warrior, Achilles, in the war. Priam himself was killed on the same night that the Greeks conquered Troy.

Prometheus: Greek hero who stole fire from heaven and gave it to mankind. This angered the gods, and so Zeus chained Prometheus to a rock. Each day his liver was eaten by a vulture, and each night the liver grew back. After a long time, Hercules slew the vulture and freed Prometheus.

Proteus: An old man who could foretell the future. Proteus was a favorite of Poseidon, the sea god, and tended his sea calves. Anyone who could catch Proteus and hold him could make him predict the future. Since the old man could change himself into any shape, (lion, fire, dragon, etc.) only the bravest could hold him and have their futures told.

Psyche: See the article on Cupid and Psyche.

Pygmalion: A king of Cyprus who fell in love with a statue that he had sculpted. The statue, called Galatea, was of a beautiful young woman, and Pygmalion adorned it with fine clothes and jewelry. He asked Venus, the goddess of love, to give him a wife as beautiful as the statue, and one day he discovered that the statue had become a real woman. Pygmalion and Galatea were married.

Pylades: See the article on Clytemnestra.

Pyrrha: See the article on Deucalion and Pyrrha.

Pythias: See the article on Damon and Pythias.

Satyrs: Minor gods, with pointed ears and the feet and tails of goats, who lived in woods and mountains. Young ones were handsome young men with short horns on their foreheads, but older ones were bearded, ugly, and wrinkled.
The satyrs attended Dionysus, god of wine and revelry. (Roman fauns were much like the Greek satyrs.)

Scylla and Charybdis: Fearful sea monsters who lived in the Strait of Messina, between Sicily and Italy. Scylla, once a beautiful girl, had been changed by the enchantress Circe into a six-headed monster and lived in a cave on a high cliff.

Each head was on a long neck which could reach out and grab sailors from passing ships. Charybdis lived underwater and sucked in great waves of water, making whirlpools that trapped ships.

Sailors were afraid of passing between Scylia and Charybdis, because coming too close to either could bring disaster.

Senele: See the article on Dionysus.

Sibyl: A woman who could foretell the future was called a sibyl. The Greeks and Romans thought these women were inspired by the gods. The Cumaean sibyl (who lived in a cave at Cumae, near Naples in Italy) was said to have written nine books that foretold the future of the city of Rome. When the Roman king Tarquin refused to buy the books from her, she burned three and offered the rest at the same high price. He refused again, and once more she burned three of the books. Tarquin finally paid the original price for the three remaining books, which were consulted until they were destroyed in a fire at a temple on Rome's Capitoline Hill.

Sirens: Three sea nymphs whose music was so beautiful that it lured passing sailors to the island where the Sirens lived, and the ships would crash on the rocks. Jason and the Argonauts listened to the music of Orpheus' lyre to avoid the Sirens' song. Odysseus and his men passed the Sirens' island safely because Odysseus had his men stuff their ears with wax and then tie him to the mast. In that way, he could hear the beautiful song without endangering the ship.

Sphinx: A monster with the body of a lion, head of a woman (or a pharaoh), wings of a bird, and tail of a serpent. It lived on a high rock near the city of Thebes, in Greece. Whenever people passed by, the Sphinx would ask a riddle, and it would eat anyone who could not answer the riddle. When Oedipus finally answered the riddle, the Sphinx killed itself.

The riddle asked, "What has four feet, three feet, and two feet, and is weakest when it has the most feet?" Oedipus answered: "Man. When he is a baby he crawls on four feet and is weakest. As an adult, he walks on two feet. He walks on three when old and using a cane for assistance."

Styx: The most important river in Hades, the underworld. For a fee, Charon the ferryman would carry souls of the dead across the Styx.

There was also a waterfall in northern Greece called the Styx, and the ancient Greeks believed that the entrance to Hades was behind the waterfall.

Swan: Swans were associated with the god Apollo. According to some legends, he was turned into a swan.

Talos: See the article on Europa.

Tarquin: See the article on sibyl.

Terpsichore: The muse of dancing.

Thalia: The muse of comedy.

Theseus: Son of Aegeus, a king of Athens. He killed the Minotaur of King Minos on Crete. (See Labyrinth.)

On his way back to Athens, Theseus was supposed to have flown a white flag to signify to his father that all was well. He forgot to do this, and his father assumed that Theseus had been killed by the Minotaur. In his sorrow, Aegeus killed himself before the ship landed. Theseus became the new king.

Theseus had several other adventures, including fighting against the Amazons. In the end, he was killed by King Lycomedes of Scyros.

Titans: Six giants and six giantesses, the sons and daughters of Uranus (heaven) and Gaea (earth). In the beginning, they all lived in heaven. One of them, Cronos, overthrew his father and married his sister, Rhea. They had many children, including Zeus, and Cronos came to fear that one of the children would kill him as he had done his father. In one story, Cronos swallowed all his children so none could overthrow him, but Zeus alone escaped. When Zeus grew up, he conquered the Titans and became king of heaven.

Also see the articles on Atlas and Zeus.

Tithonus: See the article on Eos.

Triton: Son of the chief god of the sea (Poseidon), and a sea god himself, Triton lived in a golden palace at the bottom of the ocean. It was said that he could calm a stormy sea by blowing his horn, made of a sea shell.

Trojan War: War fought between the Greeks and the people of Troy some 3,000 years ago.

For many years (in recent times), the war was thought of as strictly mythical by most people, although a few believed there was some fact behind the legend. In the 1870s, a German archaeologist named Heinrich Schliemann excavated a site that is now generally accepted as the ruins of the real city of Troy.

The story of the war comes chiefly from the ancient

writing of Homer, a Greek poet who seems to have combined fact and myth in his work, the *Iliad* (so called because Ilium was the Greek name for Troy.) While the resulting account of the war and its causes may not provide historically accurate information, it has fascinated generations, for hundreds of years.

In a way, the Trojan War began because a goddess named Eris was not invited to a party. (See the article on Eris.) Perhaps the war began because the goddess Aphrodite chose a strange way to reward Paris (son of King Priam of Troy) for doing her a favor. (See the article on Paris.)

A major reason for the war (according to Homer) was that Paris stole Helen, the most beautiful woman in the world, from her husband Menelaus, a Greek prince. Menelaus enlisted the help of his brother Agamemnon, a Greek king, and together with the great warriors Achilles and Odysseus (same as Ulysses) set out to rescue Helen from Troy.

For about ten years, the Greeks and Trojans held a series of indecisive battles. It was said that the Trojans could not be defeated as long as the mighty warrior Hector (also a son of King Priam) lived. Then Hector was killed by Achilles. Shortly afterward, the Greeks tricked the Trojans with the wooden horse, and King Priam was killed when Troy fell.

For more detailed accounts, see the articles on Achilles, Agamemnon, Ajax, Circe, Clytemnestra, Electra, Hector, the Iliad, the Odyssey, Priam, and Scylla and Charybdis.

Twelve Labors: See the article on Hercules.

Urania: The muse of astronomy.

Uranus: Father of the giant Titans. He was heaven, and he married Gaea (the earth), and their children became the chief gods. He was overthrown by his son Cronos. See the article on the Titans.

Zeus: King of the Greek gods. (Roman Jupiter.) Zeus was the son of Cronos, a Titan. In one story, Cronos swallowed all his children so none could overthrow him, but Zeus alone escaped and killed him. In another version, Zeus and his brothers revolted against Cronos and split up the world. Poseidon (Roman Neptune) ruled the sea, Hades (Roman Pluto) ruled the underworld, and Zeus ruled the heavens and earth.

Zeus married Hera (Roman Juno). Their children were Ares (Roman Mars), Hephaestus (Roman Vulcan), and Hebe. Athena, also called Pallas Athena, sprang fully grown and armed from the forehead of Zeus.

The king of the gods ruled from atop Mount Olympus. Using thunder and lightning as his weapons, Zeus protected the family and the state, punished criminals, and ruled the destiny of each man.

Though a god, Zeus was hardly a perfect being. For instance, he had a fondness for human women (much to the dismay of his wife, Hera), and would occasionally change his form in order to be with them. He turned himself into a swan to court the Greek princess Leda. See also the article on Io.

Roman Gods and Goddesses

The Roman civilization arose after the greatness of the Greeks had subsided. The Romans adopted most of the Greek gods, changing their names, but keeping their major characteristics.

In the following listing of the Roman deities, only the Greek equivalent is given, unless the Romans added their own twist to the legend and made it their own. In these instances, the story of the character is told.

Achates: Faithful friend and companion of Aeneas. See the article on Aeneas.

Aeneas: Hero told of in the *Aeneid by* the Roman poet Virgil. Aeneas was a Trojan, son of Achilles and Venus. After the fall of Troy, he escaped, spent some time with Dido at Carthage, and then ventured to Italy. His descendants founded Rome.

Apollo: Greek Apollo, also. God of the sun.

Augurs: Sixteen Roman men appointed to discover the wishes of the gods. Before making any big decision, the government would call upon the augurs to decide whether it was a good or bad time to act. Sometimes the augurs would sacrifice animals, looking for a sign from the gods. Sometimes they tried to read signs from acts of nature. One such act that the augurs looked at was lightning—if the lightning flashed from left to right in the sky, it was a good sign; right to left was bad.

Bacchus: Greek Dionysus. God of wine.

Ceres: Greek Demeter. Goddess of agriculture.

Cupid and Psyche: Cupid (Greek Eros) was the son of Venus, goddess of beauty; Psyche was the daughter of a king. She was so beautiful that people admired her beauty more than that of Venus, and this enraged the goddess. Venus ordered Cupid to use his magic arrows to make Psyche fall in love with some awful creature, but, when Cupid saw the princess, he fell in love with her and soon married her.
Telling Psyche that she must never see his face, Cupid came to her only at night. One night, after he had fallen asleep, she lit a lamp and looked at the handsome god. He awoke and, telling her that her distrust showed a lack of love, left her.

    Heartbroken, Psyche searched vainly for Cupid and finally went to Venus for help. The goddess of beauty gave her several seemingly impossible tasks to perform, but Psyche succeeded each time, secretly aided by a reed, a tower, an eagle, and finally by Cupid himself. Pleased with Psyche's ingenuity and perseverance, Zeus rewarded her with immortality.

Diana: Greek Artemis. Goddess of hunting.

Dido: Queen (and, some say, founder) of Carthage. In Virgil's *Aeneid,* the Trojan prince Aeneas was shipwrecked near her city. Dido fell in love with him and, when he left her, killed herself.

Dis: Greek Pluto. Ruled Hades with his wife Proserpine (Greek Persephone).

Faun: Similar to the Greek satyr.

Flora: Goddess of flowers and of springtime. In her honor, Romans celebrated a festival called the Floralia in the spring.

Janus: Almost as important as Jupiter, Janus stood for the beginning of everything. Guardian of heaven and of all gates and doors, Janus is pictured with two faces, supposedly so he could see what was coming *and* going.

Juno: Greek Hera. Chief goddess and wife of Jupiter (Greek Zeus).

Jupiter: Greek Zeus. Chief god.

Juventas: Greek Hebe. Handmaiden to the gods.

Lares and Penates: Lar was the ancestor and protector of the family, and the penates were gods that protected the family's goods. It was customary for each family to have a small statue of the lar placed between two statues of the penates, and to offer gifts and food to each little statue on New Year's Day, when Vesta, goddess of the home and hearth, was honored.

Mars: Greek Ares. God of war.

Mercury: Greek Hermes. Messenger god.

Minerva: Greek Athena. Goddess of wisdom.

Neptune: Greek Poseidon. God of the sea.

Romulus and Remus: Legendary founders of Rome. Twin sons of the war god Mars and Rhea Silvia, daughter of king Numitor. Numitor's younger brother seized his throne and ordered the baby boys thrown into the Tiber River. They were saved and fed by a mother wolf until a shepherd found them and took them for his own.

Once grown, Romulus and Remus restored Numitor to the throne. They decided to build a city on the banks of the Tiber, and agreed to let the gods decide which of them would name the city. Looking to the sky for a sign, Remus counted six vultures, but Romulus was favored when he saw twelve vultures. He named the city after himself, calling it Rome. Angered at losing to Romulus, Remus jumped over the city walls to show how poorly the city was defended. In a terrible fight that ensued, Romulus killed his brother. Romulus thus became the first sole ruler of Rome. (By coincidence, the last ruler of the real Roman Empire was named Romulus Augustulus.)

Saturn: God of agriculture and father of Ceres, goddess of agriculture. He ruled the world in a Golden Age of peace and bounty. In December of each year, Romans honored Saturn with a feast called the Saturnalia. (Associated with the Greek Cronus.)

Venus: Greek Aphrodite. Goddess of love.

Vesta: Greek Hestia. Goddess of the hearth fire. Rome had one large temple to Vesta, in which a fire was kept burning continuously. The fire itself represented the goddess Vesta, and six unmarried women (called the vestal virgins) were responsible for keeping the fire going.

Chosen from daughters (from six to ten years old) of free Roman citizens, each of the vestal virgins served for thirty years. Though the virgins commanded great respect, if they broke their vow of chastity, they were punished by being buried alive.

Vulcan: Greek Hephaestus. God of fire.

All Around the World

In this section, we include some of the more popular gods and goddesses, legends and fables, gleaned from nations around the world.

Many of the characters and events that are here called "Norse" are also of Germanic and Scandinavian origin. As is true throughout the book, characters and events are referred to here as if they were indeed "real." Those entries that concern actual people, such as Abelard and Heloise, are noted as such in the article.

Abelard and Heloise: A true love story. Peter Abelard, born in France in 1079 AD, was a scholar and school teacher who fell in love with Heloise when she was his pupil. Her uncle, Fulbert, was a head of the Cathedral of Notre Dame in Paris, and he did not approve of Abelard. After the pair were secretly married, Fulbert hired a gang of thugs to attack and mutilate Abelard.

The brutal attack left Abelard physically and mentally scarred; he felt that he was no longer suitable to be the husband of Heloise. He became a monk at the monastery of St. Denis. Heloise, distraught, became an abbess in a convent. They wrote beautiful letters to each other for the rest of their lives. Abelard and Heloise are buried together in Paris.

King Arthur: A king in ancient England who, with his Knights of the Round Table, had great adventures. Son of a king called Uther Pendragon, he was given as a baby to a friendly knight to be raised. Uther died when Arthur was a young man, and the man who would succeed Uther would be the one who pulled an enchanted sword from a stone in which it was embedded. Many men tried to pull out the sword and failed. Young Arthur, still unaware that he was the king's son, took the sword and pulled it quite easily out of the stone. He was proclaimed the new king.

Arthur won the fair Guinevere and made her his queen. He was counseled by Merlin, a great magician. In his fine castle in a wonderful place called Camelot, he had a great round table built, where he and his knights could sit in discussion as equals, with no one at the head of the table. Most Knights of the Round Table, including Sir Lancelot, Sir Galahad, Sir Gawain, Sir Bedivere, and Sir Percival, were loyal, honest, courteous, and brave. One of them, Sir Mordred, was an evil man, who finally wounded King Arthur and caused his death.

Dying, Arthur was placed on a barge and set adrift. A group of fairies then took him to a wonderful place called Avalon, where he would stay until, some day, England was in need of him.

There may have been a real King Arthur, but most of the stories about him are fiction.

Asgaard, or Aesir: Home of the Norse gods. A place of luxurious palaces and halls, its most beautiful one was Valhalla, the hall of dead heroes.

Astarte: Chief goddess of several ancient peoples, most notably the Assyrians and Phoenicians. Astarte was often pictured as a cow or as a woman with a cow's head.

Balder: Norse god of light, son of Odin and Frigga. Wanting to protect her son, Frigga made everyone and everything (except the mistletoe plant) agree not to hurt him. At length, a dart made of mistletoe struck Balder and killed him. See the article on Loki.

Blondel: A favorite minstrel of Richard the Lionhearted. After the Third Crusade, Richard was captured and held for ransom by the king of Austria. Blondel went from castle to castle, standing outside and singing a song that only Richard would know. At the Castle of Durrenstein, he began singing and, from a dungeon, Richard joined in. Blondel took the news to England, and Richard was saved. There was a real minstrel named Blondel, but the legend of his saving Richard is fictional.

Brodie, Steve: A New York city saloon-keeper of the late 1800's. In 1886, Brodie claimed that he had jumped from the Brooklyn Bridge into the East River, a drop of 140 feet. Few people believed Brodie, but taking a big risk is still called, "pulling a Brodie."

Bunyan, Paul: An imaginary hero of the logging camps of northwestern America. The stories of the giant lumberjack and his blue ox started over a hundred years ago. The ox, Babe, was so big that it measured "42 ax handles and a plug of chewing tobacco between the horns."
   Bunyan is said to have lived in the time between the Winter of the Blue Snow and the Spring That the Rain Came Up From China.

Cophetua: An African king in a poem written hundreds of years ago. King Cophetua, rich and powerful, fell in love with a poor beggar girl named Penelophon. In spite of the differences in their status, they were married, proving the power of love.

Crossbill: A bird of the canary family whose bill is twisted. According to legend, when Jesus was crucified, the birds tried so hard to pull the nails out of the cross that their bills became twisted.

Dragon: Fire-breathing monster with a long body, wings like a bird, scales like a reptile, claws like an eagle, and a tail like an alligator. The dragon figured in the myths of many cultures; it is the national emblem of Wales and ancient China.

In legend, St. George, the patron saint of England, slew a dragon.

Eddas: Collections of stories, in the form of songs or poems, about the ancient Norwegian gods and goddesses, or about the beginnings of the earth and its inhabitants. Most were written in Iceland in the 13th century.

Everyman: Title character of a 15th century English morality play. Everyman is summoned by Death and tries to persuade his friends—including Beauty, Kindred, Good Deeds and Worldly Goods—to go with him. In the end, the only one he takes with him is Good Deeds.

Fairy: Being with magical powers in the folklore of various lands. Most types were depicted as capricious and mischievous, but some were generous and caring. The Irish leprechauns were tiny men who hoarded gold, while the German Lorelei was a beautiful enchantress, and others were man-eating giants, or ogres. Other fairies were the Scandinavian troll, the English Pixie, the Arabic jinni, and the Germanic elf.

Fingal, or Finn MacCumhal (pronounced ma-cool): Hero of old folk stories of Ireland and Scotland. A man of that name did exist, but the tales of his doings are largely fictional. In the year 250, the king made Fingal the head of an army called the

Fianna, who roamed the countryside. One of the band stole his girl, Grania, and he searched all of Ireland and Scotland before finding and killing the man.

Part of the legend holds that Fingal built the Giant's Causeway as a road for giants crossing between Ireland and Scotland. The Giant's Causeway really exists; it is a peculiar formation of tall rock columns on the northeastern coast of Ireland.

Frey and Freya: In Morse mythology, brother and sister god and goddess of love, peace, marriage, and all things associated with the growing of plants: sun, rain, and soil.
Freya was the wife of Odin and chief goddess. She, as the most beautiful of the goddesses, was much sought after by a race of evil giants.

Frey owned a magic boat, big enough to hold gods and armies, yet able to be folded so small that it could be carried in a pocket. See the article on Frigga.

Frigga: Norse mother goddess and wife of Odin. She was goddess of the household and marriage. Later, she came to be called Freya and became goddess of the earth.

Gambrinus: Mythical king of Flanders (an area now divided between Belgium and the Netherlands). Considered the patron saint of drinking in Germany, he was depicted as a jolly fat man, usually sitting atop a huge barrel of beer, merrily quaffing a foaming mug of the brew.

Gilgamesh: The greatest hero of Babylonian and Assyrian (Persian) mythology. Gilgamesh was so handsome, wise, and daring that all the women loved him and all the men were jealous. The men asked the goddess Ishtar to create a rival for him. Ishtar relegated the task to another goddess, Aruru, who made Engidu the rival. Engidu was handsome and wise, big and strong, and knew everything about the past and future. However, he had the body of a bull with the chest and head of a man, and he much preferred to wander the forest in the company of animals to being with people.

Gilgamesh and Engidu were destined to fight, and when they did, the conflict was so tremendous that people felt the earth shake miles away. Gilgamesh won at length, and the two became friends thereafter, going on to great adventures together.

When Engidu became ill and died, Gilgamesh learned to fear death. He began to search for the Tree of Life, a magic tree that could make him immortal. The search lasted for many years and led him into great adventures.

Gnome: In fairy tales, a spirit who lives underground and guards great treasures. In appearance, they are usually little, ugly, gray men with pointed beards and long pointed caps.

Lady Godiva: The legend of Lady Godiva is loosely based on the true story of a real English lady. In Coventry, England, nearly a thousand years ago, Lord Leofric was forcing the townspeople to pay high taxes. His wife, Lady Godiva, begged him to lower the taxes, and he said, sarcastically, that he would do that when she rode through the town naked! So she did, with just her long hair to cover her.

Out of respect for the lady, the townspeople closed their shutters as she rode by—all (according to legend) but one. Tom the tailor peeped through his window and was struck blind, and was known ever after as "Peeping Tom."

Gremlin: A small fairy-like creature who causes trouble, particularly with machinery. In World War II it became a popular joke among pilots to blame any mechanical problem on gremlins.

Groundhog Day: An old legend says that the groundhog (or woodchuck) gives up its winter hibernation and comes out of its burrow on Candlemas Day, the second of February. If the groundhog sees its shadow (if the sun is shining), winter weather will continue for six more weeks.

Holy Grail: The cup that Jesus drank from during the Last Supper (a grail is a cup). Legend has it that the Grail was given to Joseph of Arimathea, the man who gave up his own grave so that Jesus could be properly buried. The Holy Grail, which had magical powers, was taken to England, where it was guarded for many years by Joseph's descendants. At one point, it fell into the possession of a man who was unworthy of owning it, being an evil person. It was then that the Grail disappeared, and it was held that only a worthy descendant of Joseph of Aramithea would ever be able to find it.

   The Grail legend became interwoven with that of King Arthur and his Knights of the Round Table, who made the quest for the Holy Grail one of their great missions. Sir Galahad was the purest of the knights and was a descendant of Joseph. After great adventures, Galahad is said to have finally found the Grail.

Isis: An Egyptian nature goddess, wife of Osiris and mother of Horus. It is thought that, early on, Isis and Osiris were the only gods worshipped by the ancient Egyptians, but other deities were added as time passed.

   Worship of Isis passed to the ancient Greeks, who came to call her Demeter. Later still, the Romans adopted Isis and built temples to her.

Juggernaut: A huge statue representing one form taken by the Hindu god Vishnu. Kept in a temple at Puri, India, the statue was moved each year to the summer home of the god, about a mile away. It was pushed on a huge cart by hundreds of Hindu followers who made the pilgrimage to Puri as a form of worship. Many people fell while pushing the cart and were crushed beneath the huge wheels. For this reason, the term "juggernaut" has come to stand for any force that keeps moving straight ahead, regardless of the consequences.

Loki: A god-like giant known for his trickery in Norse mythology. He could do good deeds, but usually as part of some evil scheme. He constantly sought ways to overthrow the gods of Asgard. Loki tricked one god into killing Balder, the god of light, with an arrow made of mistletoe. As punishment, the other gods tied him with ten chains to a great rock and hung a serpent over his head. Earthquakes were supposed to have been caused by Loki's writhing, trying to free himself.

Loki had three children: Fenris the serpent, Midgard the wolf, and Hela, who was death.

Mermaid: A sea creature in the form of a beautiful woman with the tail of a fish. The folklore of many countries includes some version of the mermaid myth. Often they are pictured sitting on the shore, or a large rock on the beach, looking into a mirror, and combing their long hair. Though not always harmful, they were often said to lure men into the sea to live with them. Mermen, their male counterparts, are spoken of much less frequently.

Nibelung: A dwarf of Germanic myth. The Nibelungs possessed a great treasure of gold. One story was written as a long poem and later made into a series of operas *(The Ring of the Nibelungs,* or the *Ring Operas)* by German composer

Richard Wagner.

In the story, the hero Siegfried steals the gold and marries a girl named Kriemhild, sister of King Gunther of Burgundy. Siegfried kidnaps Brunhild, a Frankish maiden, for Gunther, and Brunhild persuades another fellow, Hagen, to kill Siegfried in revenge for her kidnapping. After the murder, Hagen takes the gold of the Nibelungs and hides it beneath the Rhine River. The widowed Kriemhild vows revenge for Siegfried's death and marries Attila, King of the Huns, assuring general mayhem from which few escape.

Odin: Chief god of Norse myth, god of war and creator of the world. He lived in Asgard with his wife, Freya. On each shoulder he carried a raven. The birds, Huggin and Munnin, whispered into Odin's ear all that they learned as they flew about the world. Huggin represented mind, and Munnin stood for memory. Some stories feature Odin with only one eye, having given up the other eye to gain more knowledge.

Odin and Frigga had many children, the greatest of whom was Thor, guardian of gods and men. Odin's palace, or hall, was called Valhalla, and it was here that the souls of brave warriors went when they died, to feast and swap stories with Odin.

Osiris: Egyptian god of the underworld, husband of Isis, and brother of Set (the evil god of the night). As god of fertility, Osiris was believed to have brought agriculture and civilization to Egypt. Pictures often show Osiris wrapped as a mummy, with a crown on his head.

Robin Hood: An English outlaw who "took from the rich and gave to the poor." Some believe that the legend is based on a real man, but others do not.

Robin lived in Sherwood Forest with his "band of merry

men," which included Friar Tuck, Little John, and Will Scarlet. In the version of the story that is most popular today, Robin Hood loved Maid Marion, a ward of King Richard the Lionhearted. While Richard was away on the Third Crusade, his brother John ruled England and taxed the people cruelly. Robin fought the tax collectors, most notably the Sheriff of Nottingham. Branded an outlaw, Robin was in constant danger, and yet risked death to participate in an archery contest to win the kiss of Maid Marion.

In a less-known tale, Robin Hood became ill and sought out a nun to be bled. In those days, people thought that letting blood out of the body would provide a cure. However, this nun was unsympathetic to the bandit, and let him bleed to death.

John and Richard were actual kings of England.

Roland: A French hero of legend, supposed nephew of Charlemagne (who was an actual emperor). In a poem called *The Song of Roland,* written about a thousand years ago, Roland and his men killed 100,000 Saracens in a terrible battle, while losing only fifty of their own warriors. Suddenly, another army of 50,000 Saracens attacked. Roland blew his horn to summon help from Charlemagne. He blew so hard that the veins of his neck burst, and he died, just before Charlemagne and his forces arrived.

Set: Egyptian god of evil and darkness, also god of the desert and of Egypt's enemies. Set was the brother of Osiris, the chief deity, who worked to spread goodness and light. In some of the stories, Set killed Osiris and was later killed himself by Horus, son of Osiris.

Valhalla: Palace hall of Odin, chief of the Norse gods. Warriors who had died bravely in battle went to Valhalla to live with Odin.

Valkyries: Nine maidens of Norse myth who attended Odin. Riding through the air on horses, they carried, into the thick of battle, Odin's orders concerning who would win and who would die. The Valkyries were also thought to be present in storm clouds.

Vampire: In legend, a corpse that rose from its grave at night to suck the blood of living men. Able to appear in human or animal form, the vampire could be killed only by driving a stake through its heart or chopping off its head with a gravedigger's shovel. It could be warded off by the smell of garlic or by the sight of a religious cross.

   The most famous of the vampire stories is a book called *Dracula*, written in 1897 by English novelist Bram Stoker.

Werewolf: A man who changes into a bloodthirsty, man-killing wolf, usually on the night of a full moon. The myth of the werewolf was especially popular during the Middle Ages, and some people of that time also believed that a wound inflicted on the wolf at night would show the next day, when the werewolf became a man again.

Witch: According to legend, a person who could perform feats of magic, such as summoning spirits for evil purposes. Not all the witches in the stories were bad, but most were. The term "witch" can refer to either a man or woman, but usually only women are called witches, while men who perform magic are referred to as "warlocks."

   Up until only a few hundred years ago, many people believed in witches, and sometimes hunted down people who were suspected of witchcraft and killed them. In Salem, Massachusetts, in 1692, several innocent women were burned at the stake because their neighbors accused them of summoning evil spirits to do mischief.

If you've found this book useful, please consider leaving a short review on Amazon. Thank you.

KNOWLEDGE *BLASTER!* Series of educational study guides:

American History
Art History
Food and Drink
Geography and Travel
Literature
Movies
Music
Mythology
Sports
Weight Training and Total Fitness
World History

Yucca Road Productions